Forward

I chose 'Puertas' for this book title, because in the translation from Spanish to English, this one word encompasses a lot of what I wanted to express. That is, one word for many definitions.

This book is for people who seek beauty, difference and magic. Who can be time travelers and old souls.

My wish is that the photographs and text will spark in them a life unremembered, the possibilities of seeing, not just looking. Of paying attention.

The magic of what happens, where your mind travels to, when you look at a photograph.

Strange how a photograph triggers my imagination and takes me away... opening all my doors.

It is only now, having found the finish for this journey, that I can remember the beginning.

Trying to put this puzzle together, piece by piece.

We never really notice the doors. The ones we go through every day. To the depot, to the train, to the bus, to the work. Somewhere very different, in another city or country, a doorway becomes an exciting adventure. And the doorway leads to it - through it. What's on the other side? This is possibly the fascination. It stands closed, secure, locked perhaps. You try the handle - not locked! Excitement builds. Dare you enter? Thrills dance deep in your belly.

Think of the new lives a door opens. For a new relationship, a new job.

When entering a door for a new job interview, as you reach for the handle, you'll say, 'Ok, it's ok, you are gonna be fine. You can do this.' Then turning the handle, we open it and there it is - the new beginning in life. Another chapter begins. Yet when we open the door, we are not consciously taking in what we are beginning.

After that, the door becomes the thing we go through, day after day, week after week, year after year. The work becomes the place we see more than family, friends, lovers.

Doors. Puertas. To keep safe. To keep out. An entry into a new journey in life. A new love, a new job, a new experience.

Closing. A chapter in life. A slamming door signifying, signalling the end of a relationship.

The Devil's Turnstile, (Prison), Amsterdam

<u>The Devil's Turnstile</u>

The job. What I did automatic for years of my life. With it came the waiting and remembering. And the locked doors. Probably to my heart, soul, hope. But I didn't know. The prison. To be able to feel anything. Now I am starting to. I am just doing, not thinking. Remembering but not much else. Trying to piece together in photographs of those days. It starts, the next part of my life, with a prison door.

Managers, handlers. Good ones do it with inspiration, love and mutual respect. Bad ones with sticks and yelling and beatings and starvation. Because all that is, in this country, illegal, intimidation was used. Bribes and threats. And the oldest trick in the book: Divide and conquer.

Workers are hired, fired or leave. Like a door of revolving ghosts. The Devil's Turnstile is about having done this all. For more than 5 years - even longer when including an art career. Round and round - its that aspect - the forever turning and getting nowhere that is infuriating. It's enough!

When did the door of opportunity become the prison?

This job, these people, they are not below me, but stand at the train halt, while I am streaking past.

Brick Wall Doorway, Amsterdam

<u>Brick Wall Doorway</u>

This place kills everything good. I'd say the way this place is run kills everything positive and productive. Like beating dead horses. Like banging a door that's bolted, locked with a bar across it, with furniture pushed up against it. Like a door with a brick wall behind it. There is nothing there. A door to revolve ghosts. What is that called? An oxymoron? A dichotomy?

Brick wall. I hate that photograph. It is a mirror, yet without reflection. But more of a mirror to my situation and feeling about it than any other. It's why I hate it. No hope there. It is what I fear will be - to find that door - the one I've searched for, knock, and it will be opened - and what's there? A brick wall!

To remember banging on it will only bloody my knuckles. I look at that photo, doorway of the brick wall. The one that represents - to me - my work, no, job I mean. It is the door that I have been banging on for almost 6 years. With my head and heart. And look what it is! A blocked, impenetrable brick wall. No wonder I got sick.

What I realised by looking at this photo, more than when I was actually there, is this was what I was banging my head against - in my job - this is what I was trying to change, attempting to transform an institution into something other than what it was. And it was me who had to change. Not perhaps a change of job, but my expectations of it, along with the expectations of the people who worked there with me. Some, no longer friends, not because of who they were, but because I'd awoken from the unrealistic idols I'd made of them. In my paranoia of the office politics and water cooler gossip, I'd seen the transparency of their smiles. Heard the lack of honest humour in their laughter - their voices dropping into a whisper of conspiratorial camaraderie and their bureaucratic listening. These, who for years were friends, -

- now became as lifeless as the plastic manikins who lay atop one another in storage. Like a genitalless orgy - arms and legs bent in frozen motion - forever.

This photo is where my fear lives. That I will try for a change - I'll give it all up - then the door will open and it will be that - a solid brick wall - and no going back.

I cannot find a door that will be the one that I just breeze through - where the winds blow warm, the sun is always shining, the love I feel lays within me, where I have friends and family around me - this is sounding like death to me.

People are happy with so little else. Why not I? This closes my throat in tears - what do they say? There is nothing as ? as a great potential. Have I that anymore? There is a little vine growing there. It's that little thing you finally see that was like an angel who stood at your shoulder whispering, *"Grow"*.

Washed in Blue, Union Station, Downtown Los Angeles, CA

<u>Washed in Blue</u>

I see myself, washed in blue. It was a sad time. I wait. I look at my reflection. I wait. The clock is ticking. The medical. My blood. I wait in a hotel in Westwood. For my brother. For the papers that come with death. For the full impact from dad's death. Suddenly I had to wait for 'it' to hit me. And I remembered yet was too busy with the busyness of death.

Dad had died a month before. Suddenly he went. As I awaited my beloved brother, I didn't know what to expect. He had dealt with all the lawyers, details and cremation. I was living in Europe so could not. I would have liked - not liked - but wanted to share that time with my brother. Waiting in hospital, packing dad's things, driving to collect them, going through them all and the snap stories that sprang up like what this photo was or that jar of Coke-a-cola bottle green beach glass or a painting dad had painted or why he kept that drawing from so long ago.

Who knows why people keep certain things? It is not always clear. And from those unclear objects, stories rise to the surface with huge question marks. Like when after mom died, dad said to me, "Look here,-" as he held up a bundle of old letters, fastened in pink yarn. The envelopes edged with stripes of red and blue - old air mail envelopes from an earlier time. "All the letters I wrote to your mom from before we were married. Tied up in pink yarn,-" he said as he shook his head, "Why on earth did she keep them?" But I knew. Not because I had been told - that secret was never shared with me, her only daughter. Yet still I knew.

I imagined her, when things got their worst, when dad yelled and she froze her retort, when he left for 2 years to work in Japan, when we kids all got too much for her and she missed him unbearably. I imagined her pulling out the bundle, neatly tied with browning corners from age, she untying the bundle and fingering them gently, letting her mind go back, far back, to before kids, when she worked as a grade school teacher in downtown Los Angeles, living with a girlfriend. She would come into their tiny apartment and collapse on the bed. Dead tired. Too tired to cook or eat. Sticky hot from LA's heat and traffic and grime.

She thinking of the love she felt for him - when they'd first met at a family gathering. He had been friends with her sister's husband - that is, dad's brother was friends with him. It was sort of all in the family, though they had never met before that somehow. I imagined her recalling how he looked to her - strong, young, so handsome. How they'd courted and finally married. Those cocktail parties, she in full white skirts and tight bodice, he in dark suit, crisp white shirt and black tie. The martinis and cigarettes and lots of jokes and laughter. Parties always filled with friends and family. Everyone talking over each other and screaming laughter at the jokes.

The romantic walks along the beach, under palm trees with sounds of palm leaves softly rustling, warm water lapping under bright full moonlight as it gently danced on the water. Twilight in Hawaii - where mom lived at the time and he visited her there. I am sure that island and her falling in love went together in her mind. The words written from so long ago - yet they stayed here in these letters, forever. Their songs of love, the promises of a family and long life together.

How could it have come to this? she must have wondered. So she kept them, until she needed to read them anew. Always at her fingertips when times got hard, how could they not?

With the uncertainties of war and his struggle for a career as artist, but he was so talented. He had to succeed. All moments from another time – and sometimes a better time. Yes, I can see why she kept them.

So were the moments I wanted to share with my brother, now that our parents had both gone. I am no longer a daughter, never a wife or mother, now only a sister. It is only he and I from our bloodline. Now that we had to stand on our own, without them. It's not easy.

Yes, he has his family, so not the same as me, a single gay woman, living on the other side of the world for so many years. I'd missed the years with them all - I'd run away to "Fame". I thought, like the songs says, "You don't know what you've got 'til it's gone". Joni was right.

So waited for my brother and the memories I'd hoped we'd trade. The roads once traveled together, now separate, that this would bring us back together. We'd have a beer and talk it all over, reliving our cherished memories, our childhood by the sea.

At Los Angeles Union Station, I waited, washed in blue.

Waiting Room, San Diego Amtrak Station, CA

<u>Waiting Room</u>

I waited. In San Diego Amtrak Station.

I've waited at Union Station in Los Angeles. In airports. In train depots. At bus stops. Reading posted signs in Italian, Spanish, Dutch, English, and Bulgarian even. I've killed time reading newspapers, magazines, paperbacks, timetables…

It's my life story. But is it? I didn't want to grow up. Working since I was a teen. Didn't want to move out - out at 19. Didn't wait for a career. Yes, I went for what I wanted. No lack of courage there. Not like some who never leave the USA. Not like some, who go off and travel the world - all of it I mean. Wondering what I would have become if I'd stayed is well, a stupid waste of time.

That waiting room is for now. For the next door to present itself. But how will I know the right door from a distraction? Still not trusting my instincts. I'm no longer naive. But now, jaded. Afraid? Yes, still.

It's like the feeling of pacing the beach, feeling the cold of the water, yet determined to swim. Telling yourself over and over you can do this. It won't be so bad - you love the sea. Still, the toes are freezing, the fresh wave chilling your ankles. When the wave comes up, you run from it - a little more inland. Yet you circle back like a shy horse, then let feet again get wet, now warming up, getting used to. Some people aren't like that - they just run toward the water and jump – no fly into the surf.

No holding back. Will I ever be that way I wonder? Absolutely no fear. I need everything always to be checked, thought over, pondered, paced over, and investigated. Until the voices work their way in and drain out the very life and enthusiasm.

If I was fearless? At what point did I just stop pacing and run into the surf, facing all fear? Was it when the tide was lower? No. It's when I saw a break in the wave set of 3. So I could run in and not get smashed by a huge wave. Not get pummeled and twisted in the strength of it. Not spun in circles and circles trying, gasping for breath - fighting for the light and sun. Finally, to somehow break the surface and come up for air. It's when I said, "Fuck it" - when I saw the break and said, 'Fuck it, you only live once,' I probably said. Then I'd run and dive in. The water hitting me feeling all the stress go. Rolling onto my back, looking up at the sky, birds above me, I'd think, what took me so long? I didn't used to be so scared of life, or did I? Not so scared as to stay where I was.

The waiting room. A lot of time spent in those. In immigration offices. In government agencies. In lawyer's offices. In train depots. In airports. Waiting to catch the train. The plane. The break.

Time, New Orleans, Louisiana

<u>Time</u>

A manikin in a store in New Orleans. She looks out with a clock above her head. It is exactly 2:22. She has a hat, old fashioned on her head with a flower on it. On her brow, shading her eyes, a veil. Her eyes look to the right. At something. What? A handsome man? Or woman? She has her chin resting on her hand.

I'm like the lady with the clock. She is curious. Looking at the passersby - chin in hand - eyes bright yet a bit lonely. Its 2:22 - will anyone come to visit her today? She looks so lovely, so stylish, will anyone notice her? She wonders why no one does. She's put on her red lips and waits in anticipation. A delicate veil over her brow. She is young and old and frozen. Like me, frozen in time.

I write, I dream, yet the dreams are of what once was, not what will be. A prison of hope trying to smile in optimism. Of looking not too hard in the mirror. Of seeing what I want to see, not what is.

I am the child who left California. On my back carrying my paintings, fresh with excitement of a new life, determined commitment in my heart, vision of success in my eyes.

This woman, she is framed by a feather boa - perfect face in a perfect frame. I was that - feminine, well-dressed, fashionable sort of - I was the girl I had dreamt of - a new life in Europe, to try with all my heart to see my artwork there.

I am that woman. She is looking to the side - toward her past, toward her years gone.

Angels Flight, Downtown Los Angeles, CA

<u>Angels Flight</u>

Bunker Hill, where I wanted to go so much with dad. All his stories of that earlier time in Los Angeles, when the smallest railroad in the world was up and running, a part of his childhood history.

It inspired in me all of the LA of old in my heart and mind. Detectives, black and white movies, paintings from the Ashcan school, the artists who painted the reality of New York and LA of that time.

My dad used to take me to LA County Museum. I still remember one painting that inspired me. It's called, the Cliff Dwellers, by George Bellows, where he captured a sweltering summer night in a city.

Here in LA, there used to be tenement buildings alongside Angels Flight. The tenement residents, who lived in run down apartments next to the tracks, traveled up and down that high hill in place of climbing the stairs that ran alongside. Their balconies overlooked the rail, the shortest in the world I think I read. The people, fat, hot, sweating on the fire escape 'balconies', chatting and gossiping with each other, probably living very poor and miserable, yet captured by this painter. He made it look, well, nostalgic, to me anyway.

The little train went up and down to deliver the weary people to their homes. It was I think, a penny to travel, or maybe free. Now it's 50 cents, giving people a sort of retro fare.

I think to me, this doorway arch to the past, is *my* past, is LA's past. Now it travels up and down surrounded by modern glass skyscrapers, fountains with marble, pavilions with sun parasols - All new, it stays a piece of the past, cut out and saved for the new. Still small, but tall and proud.

I regret that I was unable to travel up and down it with dad. He and I had spoken about it so often and he taught me so much about the history then.

My brother and I had tried to ride it one day when I'd gone back there to visit. Unfortunately, on that one day, it had been out of service.   Ironic. We will try to go next time.

I remember Dad's stories of 1940's LA, detectives and Film Noir, and when he and mom were first married, living in downtown LA. Very much in love, newly married, he working at being an artist, studying and assistant teaching at The Chouinard Art Institute, downtown.

Years later, when mom would enter my room while I was busy with my latest painting, she would pause and breathe in very deeply, taking in the smell of oil paint. Her face would get soft and fill with a dreamy sort of glow; she would go somewhere very private in her memory. When I saw this, I'd stop mixing my paint, put down my brush to take in her beauty.

She'd say once more, "Ahhhh, this smell,-" as she closed her eyes. "It reminds me so much of when your father and I were first married." I'd listen to this story, a favorite of mine.

She would talk of the late evenings on warm summer nights, the immigrant families on blankets, picnicking all around Mac Arthur Park Lake. Accordion music, softly played in the evening breeze, lights flickering on the water as little boats circled, and lovers gently danced as their children played. The beginning of their marriage. The light danced on the water as the city lights grew dark, at twilight, how the accordion music played as they drank wine and watched the children play, looking for all the world as if they were in romantic Italy.

But it was only sweltering Los Angeles, dirty and dangerous, City of Angeles, many lost.

Fire Escape in the Sky, Claremont Hotel, Westwood, CA

<u>Fire Escape in the Sky</u>

Westwood, killing time, I smoked on the hotel's patio. Nice sunny day, the patio furnished with traditional metal chairs and round table.

The desk clerk was smoking too. I struck up a conversation with him. He told me about the hotel. Built in 1935, the oldest hotel in Westwood. Still owned by the family, original owners.

It's an old building but kept new. Kept nice, impressive but simple. Original traditional furniture and art deco objects. Very authentic but with class. There is a large sitting room with a bookcase, all the touches I love. And the prices are fair.

The fire escape fascinated me. It has something Mandarin about it in its design. I suppose at the time it was a design often used. I envision every black and white film of the 40's. I wanted to go up on it, or down it, like the murderer escaping down to the street, or the thief getting away by climbing up to the roof. Why not?

It would be nice to have an apartment up there, with a view of the whole city.

Puerta Verde, Los Angeles, CA

<u>Puerta Verde</u>

Green - the colour of hope. Its new hope and life. I am green, sprung from seeds I threw 3 years ago, when I dreamed of new creativity, to saying all I can say. Green is the colour of myself, respect in myself and my new art form.

I'm deep from dark earth rich browns - deep inside the earth, pushing up, fighting for the surface, for the sun's light and warmth. For air that is fresh and clean and filled with warm breezes. I fight toward those things, up on the surface. With all that is deep inside me, I bring them to the surface, to feed on the light and air. For them to be carried from me to others, to touch and change them. To open their hearts and minds. I push through the brick wall as a green vine filled with hope. I grow as the tree, no longer questioning why I grow, it just is.

I look at la puerta verde - the green door - in the sky. A lovely spring green, the colour of hope. Art Deco French door, weathered and beaten yet wrapped in a new cloak. That of fresh sand coloured paint, with its badge of deco still intact and clean and new looking. It floats in a dazzling blue sky, clear of cloud or weather of any sort except that of a perfect day in Los Angeles.

The shadow of a tree stands strong alongside, in companionship, to encourage and speak amiably about the years they've seen together. All the changes and uprisings and silly people related violence, and now drought. They together, have seen it all. The stock market crashes, earthquakes, drive-by shootings, political changes that remain the same.

The green door speaks of a place far away - somewhere in Europe - Paris perhaps. Tall, elegant, weathered. Wrapped in the modern, but still valued.

The tree also wonders, 'Am I still valued in a drought? Will they cut me down as they've done to so many beautiful art deco architecturally magnificent creations? Will we both go by way of the disgusting mini-mall - the ugly birth child of a society with grace no more, poise no more, talent and creativity no more - only junk stuck onto more junk? New, never better. Clever, never more beautiful. Never a respectful nod to the past, a thank you for your special moment in history, a grateful bow and acknowledgement to your glory days, enough to embrace that time, respect that time, to include that time when moving forward.

Not just a wrecking ball, a wipe of the board, a cement plot sealing the history of a city. The people's past of and in a city. Must every structure be reduced to a cement box surrounded by 30 parking spaces, with a Starbucks coffee shop, a nail parlour, a dry cleaners, a 7-11, and what else? Not much at all.

Memories Gate, Laurel, Mississippi

<u>Memories Gate</u>

I remember old gates. Laurel, Mississippi. With Annie. The photo, la puerta, is scary. Like a house when I was a kid. Where the owners hung cobwebs and bouncing spiders from the trees. The place you had to walk through to knock on the door and ask, "Trick or Treat?", and you knew, in our little child's soul, they would trick you. So I wouldn't go there. Not open the little paint peeling, splinter filled gate that surrounded their property. It was always dark there, even when the moon was full.

Like the creepy man who walked past me one day, I was maybe seven? I walked alone near the scary apartment building with a pool that always glowed eerily when the light reflected off it. Just when I was about to cross his path, my eyes down with my schoolbooks across my flat chest, my protecting position.

He held up a rope, or tie that was wrapped around his fists. He held (I keep writing help) it in front of my eyes and said very clearly and quiet, so I never forgot, "I am going to kill you." He was not so old - or young - my guess now, maybe 30. He didn't laugh. I didn't run. I didn't pee myself. Just a moment, never forgotten. Still, years later I think, 'Was he the one who grabbed that girl, later, when I was in high school? They never found her.

Information, Please, Union Station, Los Angeles, CA

<u>Information, Please</u>

Information. This i a big word. So not noticed at the time.

One I'd been out of the U.S. for years. My parents had moved south of Los Angeles, years before. Since then, I'd moved from Los Angeles to Europe. During that time, I'd been back to visit as often as I could. Flying into LA, then take the train down south to see them. I'd seen a lot of Union Station over the years. One of the times I had gone there, when I was still living in Los Angeles, I called a cab to pick me up at my apartment, a roomy single in West Hollywood. He arrived, I was late.

Now you must understand, that my whole life I had seen old black and white movies. There was always the detective or someone, who was late and the taxi arrives. The character jumps into the cab and says, "Union Station and make it quick. I have a five-spot for you if you get me there in twenty minutes." I had *always* wanted to say that. Here was my chance. The cab arrives, I jump in and say, "Union Station,-" Before I can even finish he turns to me and says, "Where? Union Station, is that downtown?"

My whole body slumped in anti-climactic defeat. Ok, he was not from the city, he was from Pakistan or somewhere. But come *ON!* The image in my head was like the film reel, when caught in the projector, suddenly melted, toast and fried. Nothing was left of my fantasy. Oh well, I thought, who really was born in LA, anyway? Well, *I was!*

Another time, a few years later, 1997 I think it was, I arrived at Union Station, blurry eyed after my 11-hour flight to LA. I was beat and spacey. I walked into the station, and sat down in that shaded, forever cool waiting area. Large square comfortable 1930's style lounges, polished wood and leather with wide, welcoming arms and mint green and pale-yellow tiles lining the walls. All of it beautiful.

I had time to kill before my train, so was just looking around. I noticed the woman next to me was dressed differently. Now, for LA, that could mean anything. But her shoes were thick heeled, sensible types, not flats, which for that day were necessary - it was 80 degrees outside. More scanning, I caught in my sights a sailor. Yet he was not wearing a sailor's uniform of any I had seen. Dressed in whites with blue trim, bell bottoms, little sailor cap. More searching spotted a green uniformed soldier with straight ironed pant legs, trim short tie and a rifle over his shoulder. Yet his rifle was old, like the collector rifles my dad had on his wall. Then I saw a little girl in pigtails, white frilly dress and a big hoop. *Huh?* Yet some of the soldiers, a lot of them, wore camouflage fatigues I recognised from current newspaper articles about the new soldier. What the heck was going on? Then the AHAaaaaaa moment came.

Of course - this was Los Angeles, the land of movies. This was for a *film.* These were extras from a film, era World War 2, in costume, on break in the waiting room. Here, in 1997, some of the soldiers and sailors who milled around were not actors, but troops, going off to the 2nd Gulf War. I thought, 'They're all *so young'.* I wondered, were they scared? Talking bravado, being macho, yet actually terrified? What did they think when faced with actors in uniforms of their fathers and grandfathers? I knew my father, at age 17, had shipped out from this very station in 1944. Did the soldiers around me feel proud to go like their fathers had to fight against the Nazi's? Did they even notice?

I sat there, frozen, with two generations in uniform, milling and chatting around me. Even now I wonder, was that real? Or had I indeed gone into some sort of time warp, our two lives, my father's and mine, his life and my life merging in some time warp - our lives sliding in and out of each other's.

Prayer Moment, Union Station, Los Angeles, CA

<u>Prayer Moment</u>

I gaze upon the church. It is not really a church, but for me perhaps it is. The waiting area of Union Station, Los Angeles, is an oasis from the downtown heat. It's like a prayer. It's rose doors, hit by sunlight, shine out onto the floor. The white hazy clouded sky peeking out atop ancient ironwork, era 1930's. It's great hall, with domed, stained glass ceiling, fine wood and white washed walls. Large, lazily rotating fans hang from the ceiling, circulating the air through the dark beamed ceilings rising up above me, all simple beauty. Perhaps is why I look upon it as a church.

In art deco style, squared, leather, big and comfortable chairs squat, interconnected with each adjoining one, give a lay about, lounging feel. But really, back then, that would have been frowned upon. They were made for sitting in relaxed, but never sloppy. In fresh pressed traveling garments. Ties, hats, kid gloves all in place. Big leather bags with port stickers patterning them, tucked neatly at your feet.

Perhaps lighting a cigarette and chatting with a gentleman beside you. Remarking on the heat or expanding on where each of you was traveling to. Down south? San Diego? Or cross country, Chicago perhaps?

"I've never done that by train," I'd say, "Is it a very long journey, much to see?"

I'd be wearing a skirt to my knees. Pencil skirt it's named, with a white office type blouse, sleeves rolled up above my elbows. Wide belt. No gloves, no hat. Very Della Street. Easy traveling attire. It doesn't go much with the T-shirts, shorts and flip-flop sandals that surround me now.

I'm imagining the woman I've always wanted to be, though it's getting a bit late in life for that. It's the picture I drew when I was 17. On the platform, smoking, in the exact clothes I just said. It's titled, *Mama, I'm Leaving Now.*

And well, I did leave. Far away to Europe. But I've never dressed like that. Not here, not there. I'd like to begin with making myself into that woman. She still works hard. Why not impeccably dressed? Is that not the legacy of the women in my family? Always impeccable?

I sit on the platform now, here in Europe, train rushing towards my work, noticing women of style. I watch them touching up their makeup. Mom never would have approved. She was always dressed and made up before going out. No fixing of make up on the street did she ever allow herself.

She'd await my dad at home, lipstick on. "Always look nice for your husband," she'd tell me. I used to watch her, "Putting on her face," as she called it. She never liked me watching her. I adored her. My first love. But it made her uneasy. She'd tell me to go away. Maybe she sensed I was a little in love with her. Felt it was wrong somehow. Perhaps she knew, even before I did, that I liked women. Liked to be with women.

I still like to watch women putting on their make-up. Is there a job for that I wonder? Not as a make-up artist but perhaps as photographer of that whole woman's world. The gossiping and chatting women do in women's lounges, in powder rooms, in kitchens, on patios.

People in general interest me too. I imagine myself, traveling by train, photographing people in the lounge car or out of my window. Exploring towns and their individuality by day, working on the photographs by night, writing my feelings and observations. A traveling...what?

Mostly I find it interesting to chat with people. Their stories are so diverse and often so brave. Like the time I sat across from an Hispanic woman on a train to LA from San Diego. Her young son quietly played with some toy - not a phone - there were no mobiles in those days, while her baby lounged in her lap.

At one point, the boy needed to use the toilet. She looked at me, sized me up as trustworthy, and asked me to hold her baby so she could take her son to the toilet. I smiled to put her at ease and agreed.

Ten minutes later she still had not returned. There had been a problem with the door handle. I heard her try the handle over and over, in a panicky sort of way. At last it opened and she emerged, her brown face lined with stress. She was much relieved to see I had not absconded with her baby. She sat again across from me and started chatting. Her story was fascinating, bold and dangerous as hell.

Years ago, she had come across the mountains from Mexico, illegally. I pictured the signboards I'd seen along the freeway near San Diego, warning, 'Caution, people crossing' or something like that, with the image of a mother literally running across the freeway, child in hand flying next to her. Running across the six-lane freeway!

That sign, a picture worth a thousand words, was the life she was telling me. Running, scared, from police, from border guards, running with her child and the group of strangers she came with. Led by someone she didn't know, who had taken her money to 'guide' 'her across the border. But would he? Or would he leave her abandoned in the desert heat to die with her child? To be left at night, the coyotes baying and only darkness, no light, no moon, no one to help her. She had to have been asking if it was worth it. Or perhaps she was only with her God that night. The trust, the faith, I cannot imagine. Not at all.

My ancestors came to America for a better life. The Jewish Italians, to escape Nazi tyranny and on my Irish side, to escape the potato famine.

So, many years later, I left for Europe. Not for survival, as they had done, but to live my dream. At the time I had left LA, women were not getting any opportunities with the galleries for exhibiting their work. I'd set off to be an artist living and working in Europe.

Now I can imagine a better life in America, having left it. For different reasons. For remembering the mountains and sea. My people, my country. My language.

I feel sadness and longing in my heart. Much different than the pull of the dream of my youth. Then full of hopeful, no *defiant* spirit, of belief in myself and my talents. The absolute and positive knowledge that I would succeed.

The spirit. I miss it. My 55-year-old body, the weight of my life here in Europe, fighting to stay here, the burdens of the decisions I've made burn sorrow in my chest. I say to myself, 'It's all part of the adventure, right?' 'Making me feel so tired.

The conflicting thoughts and emotions inside my head and heart, they're like huge baggage on my back. Like I am an over filled pack mule, bags and bags around my neck, my hooves bloody and cracked, my neck strained beyond belief. If only someone would take a sharp knife and cut the ropes, the scratching, cutting ropes that tie this all to me. Cut them and let the bags fall to the ground, left in the dust.

No more needed the winter clothes, no more needed the books of art, no more the letters from friends I no longer know, or family long dead, no longer the sculptures made from stone, no more the rolls of paintings that never sold, no more the boxes and boxes of tools no longer used, no more the glasses and china of my ancestors, no more the binders of papers of a legal struggle here, the evidence saved, 'just in case', they, the government, try yet again to throw me out of their country, no more the piles of medical records with their years of fear, no more the language tapes, textbooks or dictionaries, of a language I've never loved, liked, or warmed to. Me, a capitalist, living in a socialist system.

Capitialism. That word again. I've heard that word from so many people here. They'd all been brought up in different countries with different political systems, socialism, communism, and with different cultures. At first it was a surprise to me. Why was everyone so angry at capitalism? Growing up, I'd learned of the people who had come to America, like my ancestors, with nothing and had started their own businesses. Making good money and helping their families and their workers.

People here had nothing good to say about capitalism. It felt to me, as if my whole upbringing was getting kicked around. Like the can in the street that gets kicked by every bitter and angry person walking by, getting dented and scratched until finally someone just stomps on it and still, the flattened orb is again stomped on, kicked further down the road and finally into the gutter.

No more the pages of proof I've worked here, the C.V.'s, *resumes,* written over and over again, life as artist, as waiter, as coat hanger, as garderobe worker, as warehouse worker, as event coordinator, as volunteer.

Me, the studio renter, house renter, apartment renter. No more the pages of documents of tax payer, business owner, receipt collector, file filler, forms written in strange languages, papers and papers of another language. No more lawyers' briefs, court papers, embassy proofs and signatures, made while stressed and anxious and crazy. No more vetoed passports, ID cards, phone cards, health bills, pension papers, work and company papers, on and on and on. Rivers of papers. A rain forest destroyed for all the papers. Life in Europe. How fucking exciting. How daring. How free. How brave. How unfree I feel. How trapped my heart feels in my chest. Stress pumping with coffee and nicotine in my veins, the blood long poisoned and fighting still, some how to keep me alive.

I want to burn all of it. In the desert. All the bags and pacts - a grand cleansing from the ashes to arise, newborn. Not, as I'd thought, with new blood after a dangerous operation, but with my old blood, an artist's blood, lines from stress on my face, but with light again in my eyes.

To see my sea once more.

View of the Pacific

Pause from the Heat, Laurel, Mississippi

<u>Pause from the Heat</u>

It was more than hot there. I was sweating. I think I had been running, for the exercise. The locals must have thought I was crazy.

Why did I take a photo of those chairs I wonder now. I always liked those very American style chairs, probably from the 1940's. When you sit on them, in the shade that is, the metal is cool on your thighs. They remind me of the ones you lean back on and rock, ever so gently. Not as a rocking chair, but a springy feeling. It's really just a metal curve that is springy.

I look at this photo and think, the colour is excellent! Just the right deepness of red. Perfect shades of blue on the door frame and windows and the top too, slightly lighter. Even the cheap fake wood press board trying to look like wood, looks good here.

It's a poor house that is clear. The curtain is ripped. The paint is peeling. Yet aren't those colours exactly what has become the new old school retro look - what the expensive designers are copying? Yes, they are. The rich want to look poor. Fucking ironic.

I bet though, the rich will not have newspaper, old and yellowed with age, stuffed into the corners, into any gap, to keep the bitter Mississippi cold out and the heat in. No, the rich get their gas shipped in from the Middle East. It's paid for, in so many ways.

Here is this poor house. It's probably very clean inside, cleaner than any rich house. Because the woman who owns this house, the poor house, has pride. Pride, but no man. He's long dead. So the steps are broken and the door frame sags crooked. The grass grows fat between the pavement stones.

No man anymore to do that sort of heavy work.

When I went to that little town of Laurel, Mississippi, (two s's, two times and two 'p's '- the way I'd learnt in school)

I thought, or perhaps said to my friend, the old woman who owned the house, "You *OWN* this house?!"   It was with envy I said it. I knew only rich people owned houses. I rent my apartment still after so many years.

'56 Chevy, La Mesa, CA

<u>'56 Chevy</u>

Could be it's not one. A '56 Chevy I mean. Yet when I look at this photograph, that title jumps into my head. The stark black & white, a creamy white. The raised ironwork of the logo on the glove box. I think it says "Original". Well, if it doesn't, it should. I know little of cars, yet I can see myself in this one, even though it has a hard top. I'm strictly a convertible gal.

I had one. A '66 Cutlass convertible, banana yellow, black top. Three on the tree, as it was called. Three speeds: drive, reverse and the 3rd speed for extra power going fast on the roads and for extra energy for climbing hills. Wouldn't it be great if humans had that?

Los Angeles used to be cooler. Not in temperature, but in style. There were little pink bungalow houses called bungalow courts, built in the 1940's or 50's, 'New' apartment courtyards, that were built after World War 2, for families who worked in the city. Small, no balconies, some with fountains and high ceilings, French doors looking out onto small yards where children played. Beautiful snow-white gardenias grew on small trees or lemon trees; their scent filled the warm air.

The 1960's brought in the swimming pool - a nice place to have a drink on a warm night, watching the light play on the water. For me, it was a place to swim every day. How refreshing after work, after waiting tables in the heat all day, to dive into the cool water.

How welcoming for me, years later, to fly into Los Angeles from Europe, as the plane dropped down through the brown smog, then below to see the mountains of LA.

All the tiny blue pools all over the city, scattered like blue sapphires for this thirsty wanderer. Clustered in the little towns, nestled into the hills that slope to and from the Hollywood sign, small ones in the apartment complexes of The Valley, Culver City, West LA and the large ones flickering atop the mountains with their amazing 365-degree views from the palaces owned by movie producers and studio executives.

City of Los Angeles at night. On clear, warm summer nights I'd drive my convertible up into the hills, just to park and look out at the view. Black silhouettes of the hills. Lights scattered and twinkling, like hundreds of diamonds sprinkled onto black velvet.

The wind would barely blow. Just a warm summer night, below the stars and below still, another sort of star - that of the lights of the city. Sometimes the view would stretch right out to the sea.

Below me, cars with their yellow lights would climb up towards me, snaking and curving, their red taillights flashing only to disappear, then again back into view, then disappearing once more, going in and out of view.

As a teen, I hadn't gone there with someone to kiss or more, but alone, to look out at this beautiful city - my city. It always was, and I'd thought always would be.

She calls to me now. I get that pull at my heart, at once familiar, like a long-forgotten lover, that thrill of first sight, newly awakened, the longing still there. The hope of reconciliation circling and purring like a warm cat at my feet.

She is home to me, this city. And as I do, as I have, with a lover, I question why I ever left her. I see her so clearly. Still waiting for me.

This photograph reminds me of a few others. One is of my parents, just after they were married. It's a picture of them from out the back window of the car they were leaving to their honeymoon. Huge smiles. Black suit and tie. White gown and headdress. Veil. Eyes shining. Across the window was written, perhaps in white crayon or soapy paint, 'Just Married'.

My whole childhood I saw that photograph in their shared bathroom, their happy faces smiling up at me, standing propped between Dad s razor and Mom s red lipstick.

Another photo from the same time was one of embrace. A very tiny photograph taken at their engagement party. Again, suit and tie, mom in nice formal dress. How they dressed in those days! Full skirts, tight bodices, tasteful, groomed, smart, easy feeling. It looked so easy in that time period. Formal attire, casual, a touch of accessories, how I would like to dress, could but never do. I should be in Paris or New York for that. Or San Francisco.

The photograph was of completely cherishing one another. He, my dad, held her, not as a possession, not as an ornament, nor as a trophy wife. Not blinded by love in the way of a deer in the headlights, not like he couldn't believe his good fortune that she'd said yes. Embraced in love, but just in that moment, they were *in* that moment.

Low Water, Downtown Los Angeles, CA

Low Water

Yes, *that* bridge; the one of a thousand movies over the years. Downtown Los Angeles. The water is low now, with the drought and all. But in my life I've seen it overflowing its borders. Storming rains slashing the dirty water through the city streets, flooding the storm drains, gushing into the reservoir, in a wild frenzy crashing towards the ocean.

There seemed no relief of the rains in those years. Pounding and pummelling, breaking everything in its path like some devil's fury- furia del diablo - scooping up all the little Lost Angels, carrying them off to the sea.

"Torrential storms," the media blasted from radio and TV. "Breaking up the Santa Monica Pier," shouted the headlines in disbelief and panic. The Coast Highway became a river of floating cars, people stranded with their pitiful broken umbrellas that were just plane worn out from the wind and rain.

West of downtown, where West Channel Road curves down from Santa Monica to stop at the Coast Highway and the sea, I had driven as far as I could, but the rains created a river of floating, abandoned cars. I left my car and walked back up West Channel to Santa Monica, to a friend's apartment. I told him, "I can't get through! Can I stay here tonight?", the rain crashing down on me. Of course he took me in. Friends and strangers always rallied round each other in these storms or through the brush fires or mud slides or earthquakes.

When I was a kid, living near the canyons, after the brush fires broke out, as they did every single summer, it always used to amuse me to watch the new neighbors, who'd recently moved from New York or where ever else couples moved from, here to their little suburban home on my street. At the first line of fire on the hilltop, the one that actually was 3 ridges away but looked as though it was going to come down the hill to Sunset Blvd. (on my corner) in 5 minutes, well those New Yorkers would have their car packed with all their worldly belongings, kids and suitcases in back, boxes tied on the roof, with looks of terror on their faces. They'd be off, back to New York, 5 minutes after they'd just moved in. We'd laugh and say, "Well, well, look who's moving out. Chicken! Can't take it huh? Good riddance!"

Same to Europeans who came every summer, in shorts and their white legs with black hairs and fancy polished black shoes with brown socks. They'd drive up to us and ask, "Where's the beach?" And we'd smile and point, directing them toward downtown LA. HA! Privileged beach brats? Not really. We grew up there when the houses were cheaper because the beach was so far from the city center; no one wanted to live there.

My friends lived on the corner with their divorced mothers and siblings. Working mothers. A lot of divorce in those days. The 1960's. A lot of divorced fathers coming around only a few times a year. I remember a father showing up dressed as a cop, because he was working as an extra on a film.

In the late 1950's, my dad paid $40,000 for a house that 40 years later would be resold for $400,00. The home was deceptively large.

From the street, looking like a simple little two bedroom. You walked through a little open garden. Opening the door - or if you forgot your key, there was always one under the mat - you walked into a small dining room, with a good size kitchen on the right.

Rooms of my brother and mine were adjacent on the same floor, with a small bath between them. The top floor then dropped off into a sunken living room. The old staircase with wobbly hand rail, probably from us kids sliding down it, had 13 stairs. There was a simple fireplace and piano, couch and chairs, and a patio could be seen through sliding glass doors. To the left a small bar had been built into the area next to my parent's room. The bar was the hit of parties, small but well stocked, clearly with masculinity present.

The bar was built by my father, black washed weathered wood with grass matting wrapped around it, echoing the Tikki bars that were so popular in the 1940's.

There was dark corkboard on the wall behind it, which held my father's civil and revolutionary war relics- swords and rifles. My parents rooms were closed off with white sliding shutter doors, and beyond them, a place to work on projects. My father had also built a small photographic darkroom.

Outside, a small yard, where for years grew huge tall Eucalyptus trees. Until they finally threatened to topple on the house, so were cut down, along with the little treehouse, the one I'd inherited from my older brother.
Behind that, a small garage where my brother could be heard every weekend cursing, swearing and restoring his beloved 1960's Porsche Spider, a love affaire that for lasted years.
This area nestled up to the alley and the view I had as a kid from my window. Lining the alley were little apartments, simple and cheap for that area, mostly rented to single moms, their current boyfriend and a kid or two.   Out front there was a big tree, one that every summer dripped with fuzzy black caterpillars that turned into butterflies. I heard butterflies live only one day. Imagine if people only had one day of life - would they be texting on their phones I wonder?
That house held the whole neighborhood. It was the place to come to. Kids rode up on their Sting Ray bikes. No helmets or shoes.

They'd come just to hang out or play with the toys my dad brought home from work. He worked at that time in advertising for Mattel toys. Barbie dolls, remember? 1965 Barbie dolls. Heavy on the eyeliner, lipstick and pump high-heels - these for us to play with at dad's request. He was then working as a film director and wanted to see how we girls played with the toys. No, he was not some perve, it was his work and he was great at it. Hell, Barbies are still selling aren't'they?
Barbies were "born 'in my birth year - 1959. I read they were 'Modeled after', (read stolen) from a French doll, a tramp named Lulu. Apparently, Mrs. Mattel Toys had seen the doll in France and suggested it to her husband.   The rest as they say, is history

Va Va Varoom - Tattooed Chica, La Mesa, CA

<u>Va Va Varoom - Tattooed Chica</u>

1958. "La Bamba" blasts on the tiny tin speakers of a dual dial car radio. Deep blue metal polished with love and muscle to a perfect reflexion of the clear blue East Los Angeles sky.

It's beyond hot. No breeze blows through the canyons. Steam rises off the jet-black pavement melting in the heat.

The lucky chica design swirls silver on the ivory white steering wheel, mirroring in black, a tattoo scratched onto a brown arm. "La Bamba" pulses in beat on the 2 dial radio, Spanish station as fingers snap, a cigarette lighted, a pass of palm to slick backed hair.

All dials are set to GO...*VAROOM*...screams the engine, a lion's roar. Foot sinks the petal to the floor. Spotless white leather upholstery blinding in the sunlight, chrome gleaming, windows rolled down, wing windows open, mirrors side and front adjusted to glimpse the car coming up from behind. Screaming to catch the tattooed chica, fastest car on the road. Her driver, steel of nerve, veins of ice, clear of eye, tune of Spanish on smiling red lips - a wicked smile.

No zoot suit of long dead uncles, no dirty work clothes on back broken father, his eyes sad and tired. This is a new Angelina, white shirt stretching chest, woven leather band on brown wrist, Virgin of Guadalupe around slender neck, the center white striped highway rising before her.

Cactus neon green, white ivory bones of animals long dead scattered alongside, the victims of the desert, the remains of all life. Music pulsing in ear and heartbeat, tapping green painted fingernails on steering wheel, the wind whips through black hair - flowing back toward the hills. A glimpse to the mirror, eyes bright and lined and sexy. A car from behind, foot petal to metal. VA *ROOM!* it screams, leaving another's hopes in the dust.

The fire sun is setting, singing its last song, a flattening tangerine orb on the horizon, of pink sherbet red orange, cornstalk yellow, silver lining every choppy cloud, rays of climax stretching out in the desert, where every sunset is a miracle. Lizards scatter as they feel her roar past, dashing into cooling shade.

The Ocean Liner, San Diego, CA

<u>The Ocean Liner</u>

From the Amtrak station in San Diego, I saw this huge ocean liner. Just parked there. On its left, the huge palms in shadow. They sang out to me about every adventure.

I was not alone. A man stood to my right. I commented to him, "It's really something, isn't it?" "Yes,-" he agreed while he snapped a photo.

It sung to me about every adventure - all the faraway lands and tropical islands. So many she must have seen. Who would not think of dropping everything and running to her and boarding her. To be whisked away to the ends of the earth. No work, no phones. No Facebook, no internet, no boss mooching around, no traffic jams, no earth under your feet.

There, on the glass blue sea, water all around you, no one to get to you really. There would be no more lists, shopping, food to cook, no one depending on you really. There, under a million star filled nights, all patterns of astrology finally clear to you, moon smiling down, happy just to have you along. Dreams of every old black and white movie of grand farewells and ticker tape, flowers around neck and people excited in their best clothes of summer - white dresses with wind blowing their skirts. Snappy white Panama hats getting blown - hold on or they'll fly overboard into the wind! Men in white or tan fedoras, brims over their eyes and all smiles and cheering and laughter.

I pictured that when mom told me about leaving San Francisco for Hawaii in 19—? When Grampa Lou was working there during World War 2, after Pearl Harbor was bombed. Finally, the all clear was given, and he could bring his family over from the mainland to live. How excited she must have been, to be going as a teenager, or younger? To live in Honolulu, then a much less traveled destination.

To be going to school in bare feet, no shoes. To learn the hula dance and how the native women used their beautiful brown skinned hands to tell the stories of their people. To be welcomed with fresh, pure white plumeria leis, cold on your neck, pungent with sweet scent, hot wind hitting your face, the soft air of Hawaii soaking into your soul.

Imagine walking - or running as she was a teenager then - the decks of the ship, seeing luscious blue water all around. At night, flying fish cutting the water with their fins like a knife - the sunsets - my lord how like heaven they would have seemed.

The handsome deck officers in starched white uniforms - they would turn their head. She would have given them whiplash with her naive innocent beauty. Jet black hair, hazel eyes, large and looking at everything - taking it all in - as the gift that it was - a life in the islands. Ukulele music floating on the balmy breezes, palm leaves rustled nearby the soothing lapping waves at low tide - moon bathing the warm waters in silver light.

The sunsets - they must have looked to her as God in his most creatively flamboyant. Bold red slashes, gold, pink and purple watercolor washed the sky's deep blue hues. Fire of red and lavender and hot pink and canary yellow.

Stars in the millions scattered across the twilight sky like diamonds thrown by God, for her, saying, "Here child, here is your bounty. Love it and cherish it for always." She did. She gave that to us too - my brother, father and me.

The love of her first love - that of nature, in its most grand and holy, as God whispered into her ear, 'Hear me, my voice, always. I will help you through, all the years you have ahead, my voice is there to help you, to give you strength when you have no more, wisdom when you have no words, foresight when your world seems dark and without hope - listen for my voice. I will never leave you.

Well mom, he heard you as I hear you now. As the pure spirit you are. I took a little journey on that ship - that took me through all my years, back to you. These are my family talking now and I can finally hear them.

Immigrant's View, Pacific Ocean

<u>Immigrant's View</u>

The sparking ocean. Just outside this netted porthole, how fresh the water would be on my skin. To dive into that wetness. Feel the cold hit my chest and my heart jump from the shock of its cold. To swim through it. Just glide on my back looking up at the sky. Watch seagulls overhead, so free. Free yet their cries are tears. Sad tears of years of our boats they've seen - for centuries they've seen. For my arms to feel the strength swimming gives them. New muscles for a new country. My eyes feel the sting of the salt. Washing my tears away. It's so hot in here. Unbearable, here below deck. Outside the air is fresh. I smell the salt. I taste it on my tongue. The cool wind against my face. Blowing my hair into the wind.

Above the Pacific

My feet bare on the rough deck. Splinters in my skin. I don't care. The wind and the gull's cries soar into my heart. Without fear. They rise me up and into the stream. Up to the sky, to float so free.

My eyes look down. I see the boat, so tiny now. Floating on the sparkling water. I am up here- up high. Gliding through the clouds, towards the land. Over the mountains, above the trees. I cry as the gull cries. I cry for the people in the boat below. Trapped in that tiny boat, like herring in a closed, sealed tin can. Like mackerel packed into that stifling sweating, cramped, cesspool of urine and shit and sweat and tears and moaning and gasping for air. For a place to stretch arms and legs. For the wind to whip the face. For the water to wash the tears. I fly above it all now.

I am free now, here in the sky. I live in this moment of the air under my wings. I think not of where I will go. What will happen there - I live now, flying free.

Art Caged, Tropic Museum, Amsterdam

<u>Art, Caged</u>

She holds on her strait shoulders, a steel bar. From which hang three buckets/satchels. In the first one is air - the breath of life, the gift of life, that which all living things need to survive.

In the next, water. Sweet, clear, thirst-quenching water from the sky, from the rain on the mountains, seeping into the earth, and down the washes, over the falls, into the rivers, trickles of streams, branching, turning this way and that, curving and snaking the land.

The third is art. All of humanity's music, history, invention, rises up in a voice so sweet, so heartbreakingly real: a lullaby, a war cry, a shout, a whisper, a murmur, a sob, a birdsong, a sonata, churning of industry, a baby's wail, a bored yawn, a giggle, a hiccup, a cheering crowd, an angry mob, a low whistle, a sexy, purring moan.

Opening Night, Aldwytch Theater, London

<u>Opening Night</u>

The lights beacon like fingers stretching out to me. Their fingers wide to grasp, to touch, the mind and hearts of the audience. Saying welcome - let me take you out of your normal, boring life for two hours. Listen to my grand music, see my costumes sparkle of jewels and silk, dancing around my stage while they flow in perfect harmony and movement with my music - lows that touch you so deeply, highs that lift and open, making your soul soar - taking you to another time and existence. Let my drama rip your soul - grasp it in suspense, hold it there for seconds, minutes, hours - let your heart open to me - causing you to feel so full it will burst - let your throat close and tears form in your eyes - streaking your face.

The theatre is dark - so dark you cannot see your hand in front of your face, nor the person sitting beside you. It's silent - more silent than you ever heard - the hush that comes suddenly, when all the house lights go off - the suspense of that moment - all dark, silent, all breaths stop in suspense of that moment.

Then faint, very faint, so faint you wonder if it is only in your head - a quiet bar of music begins - is that music you hear? Begins like a memory of a dream as you awaken from sleep. It is one violin string - one single line, then it grows so slowly, so far away, somewhere in the distance of our memory - your memory, it builds and you begin to catch fragments and pieces and pictures in your head - then builds with a low cello - two vines intertwined and beginning a dance - the beat, far in the back, below, like a pulse, like your heart beat thrums with two - now three - dancing, playful, causing you to remember. Still, it is very dark - you could be dreaming this all. Then the pulse increases. You tap in time with your fingers on your knee. You could be quite happy just to go on, in the dark, listening to the beat of your heart, the thrill in your pulse, the dance of three, flowing through your nerves, giving them a life's blood, you no longer remembered. Something from long ago in your DNA is awakened. There, in the dark you are dreaming, you feel no one beside you. Only your memories, feel only your heartbeat, your fingertips play like white ivories of a piano, dancing on your knee.

You could go on like that - hearing, feeling, dreaming, remembering... so easy, so gentle, like rain gently washing your soul. The lights turn from blackest black, to dark grey - like the speeding up film of a sunrise. Darkness rising and light - a light from inside your soul awakening - blood pumping once more, the flowing, three are joined by two more, then another two, complex - so complex it becomes so simple - a melody of 3, 5, 7, then the horns come low, to increase the power to shake your nerves ever so slightly - then the strings, so many, yet as one voice, building and fading - a pulse in your body.

Low cellos build still more, like a solid foundation, like an army of arms to lift your soul, the strings rising up toward the sky - stretching up to the stars they carry you - to float on the air like a feather, like a breath - like birds singing as one, like a million voices crying - calling out to your soul, touching you, mankind, nature, history, - a thousand, a million histories.

All of humanity, a chorus, all their dreams and heartbreaks, all their love and desires, hopes and fear and death and life - all their gods and wars and hunger and greed and violence and blood and tears. Heart crushing boredom, eye catching glimpses of possibilities almost grasped, almost touched, just on their fingertips. The potential not realised, the dream wrestled for, a thought moved to mouth yet not spoken, a clock ticking, a train pulling out of a station, a sunrise, a smile, a sunset, laughter from far away, a dream unremembered, shouting down a dark alley, fear that grasps your heart and snatches your breath, a fist toward your face, a guilty memory, a longing for someone long dead, a picture of one yet unborn, a toast of champagne, a cheer of a homecoming, a lover's touch, a tender first kiss, a thrill of anticipation, the blow in the gut of a love long gone, the miracle of a leaf releasing it's branch, the cloud looking like a troubled face, the musical sway of trees in the wind, the miracle of first spring buds, the relief from tension from a pull off a cigarette, a new smile in a shining mirror, a fresh step from a sexy dress that fits just right, the flip of a new hair cut that catches the breeze and a stranger's eye, a flirtatious smile, a gaze held for a moment then a bit longer, the feel of purring fur denting your bedcovers, a stranger's laugh that makes you giggle, heart clasping fear of your father's angry voice, throat closing impotent humiliation from your mother's tears, a confusing internal conflict of a wave goodbye, an awe of jealousy of a soaring bird, the thrill and envy of a jaguar in full chase, the lust of a woman's perfectly curving leg, a pause of sorrow then gratitude at a passing hearse.

Ghost Doorway, Tropic Museum, Amsterdam

<u>Ghost Doorway</u>

Doorway to a doorway. The definition of a life, I guess.

Just things, in a glass case. Doors keep them locked. Safe. Precious, unhandled. This photo reflects my career. Precious objects in a case. Unseen, un-bought. Just more stuff. They took sooooo long to create. To imagine. To paint. To carve. To sell. So many expositions filled with hope. The gallery assistant telling me, "…but your work has sold more than anyone." So why, I wondered, was I not getting a price to live on? Live from?

My exhausting, blood sucking, back-breaking, heart wrenching career. I lived not. I walked through it like a ghost. Walking, talking, answering the questions, injecting the proper enthusiasms, feigning interest, smiling - (always remember to smile) Sometimes I'd think, '**This** is my *life?* Art began to feel like a demanding lover. Nothing was ever good enough for her. I got so tired of her constant seduction, doing me until I'd drop. After 35 plus years making a career as an artist, I'd had enough.

At the beginning, when a sculpture of mine was chosen to stand at the famous art fairs in London, the sort of places I used to have a job serving wine at, I'd sit for a moment and look around, taking it all in and say, **"Yes.** THIS is my life. I'd drink a toast and say to myself, "Well done, you."

Years later, with lovers who felt neglected because I was always working, not a regular 9 to 5 job, but a career, I felt I always had to justify my choice of career. It chose me, by the way, not the other way round. Is it any different for you who wants a child? Well, these are my babies. I'd shout, **"THIS IS MY LIFE!!!"**

When history finally stamps you as great, if it does, then all that you've done to do what you did, even madness and suicide, is looked upon as ok. It's so ***interesting***.

In the end I saw clearly it was no longer sustainable for me to be an artist. Society does not credit the artist enough, not like a doctor or lawyer.

When the next sculpture was asked for, ASAP, and I'd spent another weekend inside working, carving stone, wondering how to pay the bills, wondering what the fuck I was doing, bewildered, I'd quietly think to myself, '**this** is my life?' I was an artist who saw every detail yet missed the big picture.

This photograph reminds me too of little curiosity shops in Amsterdam. Chock full of all sorts of knick knacks. Junk, antiques, bits and bobs, small precious handmade jewelry, old pen tips, bottles of various colors, shapes and sizes, old cameras, tin toys, and sometimes sculptures.

Maybe they were copies of famous ones housed in European museums, perhaps only knick knacks for tourists of their time, portraits of long dead famous people, composers and the like.

But some were good, really good, and I'd wonder how they came to be here, in a side street shop, not in a museum. How many hopeful artist's work and careers ended up here? Just expensive junk. Pretty now, because it somehow lasted, someone caring enough to care for it, to hand it down.

Did some relative receive it as an inheritance in lew of money and say, "Oh god, what it this tacky thing? Can we just sell it please?" So off it went to an estate sale, or garage sale, yard sale, boot sale or street sale, finally ending up here, in this little shop.

I'm thinking now, about all the art I've made and sold or given to people. My art is out there, somewhere in the world, possibly bringing joy to someone. Pleasing people. Perhaps handed down, but cared for, embraced, seen.

I always have felt, that an art piece does not live, unless it is seen. So maybe, this long career was not for nothing.

Stage Door, London

<u>Stage Door</u>

The stage door. The Hollywood Sign of London. Where all hopes, bright and shiny, with shining eyes gaze upon their heroes. The ones they must see. On that stage. On that screen. The doorway to fame. Who dares walk through that?

Why does Hollywood have no doorway like that? Perhaps it is the Hollywood sign that beacons the young and hopeful. The lost and broken and abused. A tear catches in their throat, the gasp of hope…that beacon like a spotlight into the sky - all across America and the world. It flashes, "Come to me" It burns brighter and longer and reaches thousands not only through the sky, but to the hundreds of thousands of miles to the little, tiny back country one street towns, to the suburbs, shiny with Formica floors and dried weed centerpieces but also out through the years.

For here, unlike London, the stars shine not for one glorious night, not for one season or two, but forever. Forever and ever. Out to every generation who discover them anew.

Ah yes, the fame of it. To be a great artist. To leave your mark in history. Your babies, your art pieces. It didn't quite turn out that way did it? That midnight train to Georgia is your song now. And I have no faith woman. No faithful woman who will go there, on that train with me, home.

Unviewed Masterpiece, Rijksmuseum, Amsterdam

<u>Unviewed Masterpiece</u>

The Nightwatch, surrounded by a beautiful Greek sea blue wall, hand carved portal that embraces Greek architecture. Rust colored woodwork, red marble base at feet, sand pale wooden floors, all frame a masterpiece for all who see it, here in the heart of Europe.

Then, walking by, this guy, this wanker, blind to the greatness, he is involved, no, *intrigued by* this tiny, plastic, world in a phone. His tiny, boring, non-inclusive, non-embracing of the rest of the world, nor to the rest of the people in the painting and all around him. I wonder if he as well uses his phone in Mosques, Synagogues, and Churches.

His world is in his phone. The world can crash around him, the climate change crash tsunamis waves into him, earthquakes crack pavement before him, tornadoes blow and swirl around him, terrorists can bomb his pathway, drive by shooters machine gun patterns of bullets at his feet, - yet as long as his phone works, he's ok. His little world will crumble only when his internet connection fails, driving him mad and manic until it is fixed.

A whole new generation ripe for manipulation, exploitation, conquering, controlling. Lambs to the slaughter. But even lambs look up at their fate.

Inside, There's Life, London

<u>Inside, There's Life</u>

Solid stone looking like cake frosting. Hard yet soft and fresh as new snow. The grand entrance calls to you like a voice echoing in the repeated columns and archways two, no, threefold they call out to the passersby. The dignified yet casually relaxed, beautiful and slightly stuck up angels, lounge above you as you enter. Their wings spread as a pattern, more than as in flight. One gazing at the other, who gazes out at you. Her hand on a round disc, I know not what the meaning is - and her other hand balances a tablet of some kind on her substantial thigh.

Both angel's feet perch on the curving ground, like a swimmer balances on a smooth rock to brush sand from her feet.

Surprisingly, the first angel grasps in her left hand a tiny, standing walking man. His face is covered by her thumb. How remarkable! Is this some sort of symbolism? Perhaps signifying something about 'Mere mortals'.

The whole building announces itself as TATE BRITAIN. The trumpets blow, saying, 'Here I am! Strong, safe and filled with all the world's art. Calling out, saying, 'There is life inside these walls. See me,-' they say, "-See us - Inside, there's life. Centuries of life. Ancient queens. Common people on Parisian rain-soaked streets, dashing out of the rain. Sun washed parks with ladies in white, their parasols hiding fair white skin from the sun. Mummies and Egyptian jewels and more..."

London Tube Tunnel

London Tube Tunnel

On a hot day, it's gritty in there. The warm air rushes at you through the tunnel, signaling the train is approaching, before you ever see it.

People stand in their pre-designated spots. They know exactly where to stand, to wait. They know when the train comes to a halt, where the doors will open, because they have stood there, day after day, year after year. Never are they disappointed, never must they walk an inch up or down the platform to an open train door. They marked their territory, and no one will step into it. This is the unspoken understanding amidst Londoners.

Another unspoken understanding is not to chat. *Especially not* about the tiny mice scurrying on the tracks. No comment, even if the trains are late, as they often are. It would be un-British to comment or even to show any kind of inconvenience on their face or in their posture. This is London, where there is no need to comment on anything except perhaps the weather or the latest Cricket match scores.

The masses file in polite lines, through the turnstiles, down the moving stairs, snaking through the walking tunnels like serpents coiling into their den, some splitting off to the right, down the back stairs directly leading to the trains. Only true Londoners know the back ways - thus avoiding all cues and tourists, who's wild eyes frantically search the underground maps spread across their chest like accordions.

They are gently, or not so gently, pushed aside - this is no place to review maps, the Londoners think to themselves. One should have studied the journey beforehand and committed it to memory.

Yes, the tourists are a bore, but at least they keep the city rich – richer than the rest of Europe. The sterling is strong – no greek euros disrupting *our* way of life. As the train stops, the clusters file into their pre-designated territories - professionally sliding into the last unoccupied seat, unless there is a tourist who has very annoyingly placed his baggage there - so rude!

All faces down, gently swaying inside the over filled cars, one hand lightly grasping the shining silver poles for balance, in the other, an open book.

Suddenly, the train comes to an abrupt halt. The passengers show no emotion, no reaction to the delay. After all, this is London. Still, they are happy to explain to the tourist beside them who urgently asks, "Why has the train stopped?" They calmly reply, "Someone under the train, probably…" "Whaaat?!-" they cry in shock, which is often met with amusement. These tourists really have no idea how many people fall into the tracks, or more often, *jump*. This too, is London.

It's not all first rate musicals and world class operas. Nor lovely green parks in summer and slashing rain and sleet in winter. When the days are black with clouds, nothing keeping out the biting wind that cuts your skin and turns your gloved yet frozen hands to beet red, broken skin with purple, bulging veins, making you look older than your 96-year-old father.

On days like that, there is a sea of black umbrellas blocking your way. No black cab will stop for you, even when you hail for one - its tires sending a wave of water over you, not only onto and into your shoes, but your whole suit as well. Very unpleasant. This too is London. Most of the time, this is London.

Still, on days like today, up top on the street, though overcrowded - it's always overcrowded - this day full of sun and blue skies, the parks fill with people strolling lazily, not in such a rush - Londoners are always in a rush - the pace slows to a fraction and one has time to take in all the lovely colours of spring, the sea of bluebells, to gaze at the children floating their tiny boats in the water.

Time to stroll along the Thames, listen to Big Ben chime and admire magnificent Parliment, the pride of this side of the world. To gaze at the mighty St. Paul's Cathedral that could not be destroyed, though god knows the Nazis tried their best to do so.

Even as the screaming bouncing bettys rained down all around her, she stood tall, unscathed and defiant to their aggression. Keep calm and carry on – this is the blood that pumps in the veins of the British in general and Londoners in particular.

Ah good, the train has started again. They apparently have moved the body from the tracks. I'll not be late after all.

Puerto del Diablo, Barcelona, Spain

<u>Puerto del Diablo</u>

Of course it is. Perfectly shadowed, the inner turmoil and self-destruction.

Bordered by strange birdlike demons, with fierce claws, grabbing claws that rip flesh. Hard browed, stern faced, expressions with lifeless eyes and unyielding postures. Arms, not wings, crossing chest, giving no entry, no possibility of entry or discussion. Sure and stubborn and absolute in stone and steel and attitude. 'No entry' they say. How they perch above the gate. No possibility of entry of life or love or hope. Heart - a stone heart - closed to all. They are gatekeepers, sentries, keeping out, keeping in.

The snakes, serpents writhing, creeping, grasping the sides, human like but disgusting, they border the sides, the entrance. The iron black that cannot so well be seen, what IS there?

A nightmare barely remembered, yet still clutching the chest in fear, in lust or greed, or shame. Objects that could be buds springing new on a tree, but they are not. Above, starbursts like fireworks, that could be filling the sky with hope of a new year. But they are not. Intertwining snake like movements, that could be the serpent coiling the sword - the symbol of medical hope and trust and belief, but they are not. It is none of these things.

They are the tiny squares, little cubicles of confusion, the dichotomy of human torment. Strong, yet hopelessly baffled. Regimented agony. Good little soldiers going off to war. Faithful little workers in shades of grey, cocooned into their grey cubicles. Refugees on a boat surrounded on all sides by water. Inner turmoil of invention and destruction. Of hope and crashing defeat. A computer grid, a prison. All that is human misery is locked there. No, I dare not enter it. Nor even acknowledge it. I don't even want to touch it. All the evil of the world lives there.

It's where the ones who won't let me sleep live. Hell is fear.

Through my Father's Eyes, Dana Point, CA

<u>Through my Father's Eyes</u>

We were on a boat, my dad and I. For whale watching. We saw no whales that day, but the dolphins chased and playfully jumped in the surf behind the boat. He would gaze out at the open sea, and talk about how he always felt at home there on the sea. Ever since he was a midshipman on a battleship in World War 2.

At that time, up on the deck, he would go there for a smoke. He said he didn't really like smoking but would use it as an excuse to escape the stifling, hot quarters below.

He would stand and marvel at the absolute stillness at night, where a million stars would pattern the black sky. He said it was so calm, so still, that the flying fish would jump out of the water, which was still and flat like glass, and fly just above the water, only a few inches, their tails skimming along that water, their fins would drag along the surface and cut the water, just like a knife.

Pictures of things I would never see, but he told them to me in a way an artist would, a way that I could see through his eyes. His gifts to me.

Biblical Garden, Scottsdale, Arizona

<u>Biblical Garden</u>

I remember that day. Scorching heat. I was in Scottsdale, Arizona. My friend had wanted to find that place again, where she had been before. I, of course, had paid little attention to it at the time.

Now, like a book that finds you when you need to read it, I am clinging to this photograph like a life raft. I'm not out of the boat yet, the one I am lazily dozing in, I'm awake now and the undertow is sucking me down. I must relax into it. Not fight it. Have faith in my ability and tools to survive this tsunami.

Knock, and the door will be opened. But which door? How do you know the right door? How to know if it is the right path, and not a just distraction? Ask it says, and you will receive it. But ask what?

To give hope. I wish I was there right now. Feeling the sun burning my skin. The rocks under my boots, solid. My muscles stretching from good, honest work. In the sun and breeze, atop where I hear no one. Atop Sedona red rocks, beautiful clear blue sky. A few white puff clouds. Will I ever feel rested, refreshed, alive again, anywhere?

It is only now, having found the finish for this journey, one of hope, that I can remember the beginning. Trying to put this puzzle together, piece by piece. I feel my heart opening. Its ok that it is - it must be a spiritual opening - not some woman or tribe of young women, yet the desert is also a woman. The sea, the desert is in my blood.

The doorway is all about faith. Faith and belief in self.

My Brother, My Hero

<u>My Brother, My Hero</u>

My hero, my cheerleader, my coach, my clarity.

The one who grounds me when I'm flying crazy.

Without reproach he replies enthusiastically.

He carried a torch for me, when I thought mine had blown out.

He kept a candle burning in the window.

He has faith in me when I lose mine.

He said,

"You are perfect as you are and where you are. You have too much to give to the world to stop now."

He reminded me of my worth when I could find none.

He promised there would be a way through and there always was.

I don't know if he meant it to be religious. I don't know if I meant to take it that way.

As I once said of him, he is a man who, when he talks,

is like a floating, lazy river.

A lovely brook, complete with turns and veering off, then back to the source,

a cool and refreshing journey one needs to settle in and take time for,

for it is always worth the going.

Floating down a stream, I have to let go and be taken on.

It does no good to jump the boat.

As I flow along with him, his words are beautiful in tempo and tone.

My mind grasps on the things he says.

And I try to catch them as one would run her fingers

catch beautiful colorful leaves on the surface of the water.

To catch them, to keep them.

What I get from his words is not that he solves my problems.

He never does

Instead, he reveals to me another viewpoint.

One I'd not thought of.

I flow with him on the journey of "What if's"

When he talks I become inspired.

This is what I take away and what lifts my spirit.

To feel truly that tomorrow is another day.

That there are seeds growing, even now.

They are of worth because they are of worth to me.

And that in itself is more than enough.

That is just perfect.

Chantz Perkins has worked as an artist in many forms:

painter, sculptor, photographer, videographer and writer.

Her work has been commissioned and exhibited in Britain, Europe and the United States.

She hosts a blog, website and webshop, where quality prints of her work can be purchased.

More information can be found at:

https://artbychantz.com

https://artbychantzblog.wordpress.com

9 789083 272306